# 34 Sonnets

by T.S. Roach

Copyright © 2021 by T.S. Roach.
Foreword copyright © 2021 by Sarah Lyn Rogers
All rights reserved. Printed in the United States of America.

First edition.
ISBN 978-0-578-96021-0

Soot Sprite Books
New York, NY
www.sootspritebooks.com

T.S. Roach
www.youtube.com/channel/
UC9QvBhbuyOlXnpC3ATUEXSQ

Cover illustration by T.S. Roach.

*Dedicated to all Moneygrubs, past, present, and future* . . . . .

# 34 Sonnets

by T.S. Roach

*With annotations by Kevin Y*

Soot Sprite Books
New York

# Contents

Foreword ................................................................. i
34 Sonnets ............................................................. 1

# Foreword

T.S. Roach can't be real. That's what I thought as I read and reread the below message, sent to me via unsolicited Twitter DM in early summer 2021.

> Dear Mrs. Lyn Rogers,
>
> Thank you for flowloing [sic] my Twitter.com profile. I hope you have "appreciated" the finnancila [sic] advice vice versa which I have been presiding and that yoru [sic] welath [sic] ahs [sic] grown manifold in the time bieng. [sic]
>
> I am writng [sic] to enquire vis a vis whehter [sic] you are a real poet and if you could lok [sic] at some poems I have writen [sic]. How do you tell if/when a pome [sic] is good?
>
> Love,
> T.S. Roach

i

As someone who works in publishing, I am no stranger to odd emails. I'm also no stranger to receiving publication requests via Twitter (though I generally prefer not to). I thought, given the sheer flex of typos, that this was spam, the kind likely to ask me to wire money or send a cashier's check to a strapped-for-cash overseas prince. But there was also something familiar about the voice. I noticed the handle again, the bitmappy profile pic.

Back in December 2020, an account called @stockroachREAL had followed me on Twitter. This person retweeted an installment of my *Catapult* magazine Internet as Intimacy column, and dubbed me "today's #moneygrubofthemonth." I didn't know what this meant, but decided to play along and follow The Stockroach back. I more or less forgot about this account until I received that message.

Two days later, he followed up:

*Hello,*
*Just flolowing [sic] up.*
*Love,*
*T.S. Roach*

And then, an hour after that:

*Acutally [sic] I wanted toknow [sic] if you would be the editor for my new potery [sic] collection.*

I could have let it go. I watched myself have a what-am-I-getting-myself-into feeling. And then I watched his YouTube videos.

Where can I begin? The channel, The Stockroach OFFICIAL, is ostensibly a resource for advice on stocks, cryptocurrencies, savings, and side-hustles to help "the entire money ecosystem GROW," but the uncanny is pervasive even thirty seconds into the first video, "EPISDOE [sic] 1: WHAT IS CASSH [sic] MONEY?" The creator doth protest too much about his age, his financial successes, his many sons, while fumbling through screenshares that reveal incriminatingly labeled desktop folders, notes to self, and hot anime girls. This can't be real, I kept thinking. The videos feel like someone earnestly and repeatedly crashing a toy car into a wall, while professing to be a professional stunt driver.

What I'm saying is that they are strangely moving. *Why*, I kept asking. *Who is this for*. In video after video, The Stockroach positions himself as a generous authority, imparting something to us, the viewers, something that we need, that only he can give. But as the tautological PowerPoints and demise of a decrepit laptop progress, and the bizarre lies and conflations and glitches (Jeff Bezos equaling Steve Jobs, President Bill Joden, checking the Jow Dones) become more outlandish, The Stockroach maintains an emotional frequency of melancholy, some deep longing for genuine connection. And, below the more obvious falsehoods and misdirections, the suggestion of a hidden, inexpressible truth—one he seems unwilling to share, perhaps not even with himself.

As I fell deeper into the videos (often including original music, bizarrely well-conceived for someone who can hardly type or remember his own age) and secrets, I became obsessed with the answers to *What is he hiding* and *Is any of this real*. Then I had to wonder: *If T.S. Roach is not real, then what does that make me?* I was the one fielding his messages, weighing their import, combing through his creations for clues to their meaning. The world of the videos seemed imaginary, and yet I felt so much a part of it, almost as if I were merely some secondary character in his fictional world.

Although it felt like an entire alternate timeline had passed, really it had been only a couple of days of binge-watching at this point. I responded to T.S. Roach's message and, as politely as possible, for the sake of my mental health, declined to edit his poetry collection. Instead, I referred him to Kevin Y, a poet and essayist with connections to the micro-press Soot Sprite Books (which published the second edition of my own poetry chapbook after the first edition went out of print).

Kevin Y asked if I would write the intro to this collection. Having taken some time and space away from The Stockroach OFFICIAL YouTube channel and Twitter, I checked in with myself and found that I would. That was the last I heard from Kevin Y, who is normally punctual and responsive, and from whom the entire manuscript is due to the printer later today. I have not yet seen what Kevin Y was able to make out of T.S. Roach's manuscript. Assuming we somehow meet the deadline and this book ever actually exists, I will not have time to edit this.

I'd wanted to end this intro with a description of what this poetry collection might make you think or feel, but it's difficult to do that without having read the thing. I had hoped to offer some connection about the T.S. Roach internet persona and some truth about the "real" person, some proof that he definitely, actually *is* real.

But at some point, "real" ceases to be meaningful. Even what's factual about a person must be filtered through subjective experience—our own, and any witness's. We are always audience, even to our own experiences. Experience becomes story, a narrative we can shape for our own understanding. Sometimes we tell ourselves stories that are the only spaces where we can be the hero. Sometimes we tell ourselves stories to convince us to stay quiet, convince us that no one else will understand. And sometimes these stories, real or not, can make someone, far away and secluded and wary, feel less alone.

Maybe T.S. Roach's poetry collection will make you feel something like that. But then again, maybe not. I honestly have no idea.

Here goes, I guess.

SARAH LYN ROGERS<br>New York City, 2021

# 34 Sonnets

by T.S. Roach

*With annotations by Kevin Y*

I.

Shall I compare thee to a dollar bill?[1]
I cannot hold or fold or spend you, but
Does not the valued role that you fulfill
Make you and Money similar somewhat?
You both bring happiness when you arrive
And sadness lives wherever you're not found.
You both are that for which I daily strive—
I try real hard to keep you both around.
But wealth is even fun to give away—
By giving you can buy yourself new things,
While I would not give up a single day
Touched by the joy that being near you brings.
        You are not like to cash for I would not
        Trade you for any other thing I sought.

---

[1] The collection begins with an obvious reference to Shakespeare's Sonnet 18, perhaps the most celebrated exemplar of the form. It is a clever choice, instantly placing his work in conversation with the grand and storied tradition of sonneteering.

I once asked T.S.R., while gathering biographical information for the back cover copy and publicity materials, what he thought of Shakespeare, and the relationship between his own work and that of the old master. He responded in typically cryptic T.S. Roach fashion: "Is he the one that wrote the Mark Twain books?"

II.

My stocks are up, and yet my mood is low.
The Dow Jones[2] doesn't carry me the way
It used to do, back when the market's glow
Could warm me like the sun warms Earth each day.
My heart is empty, though my wallet's full.
The dollar bills, they nestle crinklily[3]
Inside my pocket and I feel no pull
To take them on another spending spree.
The GDP has grown and yet I shrink
Away from all responsibilities
And from my social life. I almost think
I should cut ties with my board of trustees
        For thoughts of you consume me like a fire
        That burns all wealth, leaving only desire.

---

[2] In the process of assembling this collection, we of course sent back and forth many drafts of many poems in various states of completion. In every draft of Sonnet II I received, Dow Jones was spelled "Jow Dones." I would correct the spelling, insert my editorial feedback, and send it to him for approval. When he responded, the spelling was mysteriously changed back to "Jow Dones." While I in general pride myself on not being overtly heavy-handed as an editor I felt that, in this particular instance, it would be appropriate for me to insist on the standard spelling. If T.S.R. ever reads the completed manuscript (which at this point I'm guessing he won't, more on that later), I hope he will respect my decision or at least accept my apologies.

[3] For those who are wondering, the word "crinklily" is not, according to any of the English-language dictionaries I am aware of (many of which I keep close at hand, in various editions, on my desk), a real word. I brought this issue up to T.S.R., who responded, "Don't worry, it will be."

III.

If riches were bananas I would eat
Bananas every day, rich as I am.
I'd sit each morn upon my breakfast seat
And feast upon the fruits with toast and jam.
But if love were bananas, then I would
Be too hungry to even get along.
I'd envy all the people who have good
Bananas every day like Donkey Kong.[4]
Bananas in real life are nothing more
Than yellow fruit. They do not represent
Romance or even wealth by metaphor,
So here is, more directly, what I meant:
    If it would mean you'd fall in love with me,
    I'd give up fruit for all eternity.

---

[4] Donkey Kong is, as I learned through my research, a reference to a muscular, ape-like character from the Super Mario Bros. franchise of video games and related media. Bananas comprise a recurring motif in many of D.K.'s "platformer" style video games. I am consistently awed by T.S.R.'s ability to include references both to classic literature (Shakespeare) and contemporary youth culture (*Super Mario Bros.*) in a single volume. In a way, this collection of sonnets is itself a kind of "platformer," leaping from allusion to allusion in nimble literary style.

IV.

The hunger strikes upon the midnight hour
And draws me from the warmness of my bed.
I open up the cab'net, seeing flour
And nothing else, no cereal or bread.
The light inside the fridge a-flickers on
And off again with something that had been[5]
A dinner once, (An omelette? Or a flan?)
Lit up and moldy in its little tin.
The microwave still smells of yesterday's
Sweet supper from a box of Lean Cuisine
But not a crumb is left for me to graze
My lips against. The plates have been wiped clean.
    I wish Mom would buy groceries for the kitchen
    If I had money, I would gladly pitch in.

---

[5] I was initially hesitant to include this poem. It was actually sent to me in a document entitled "unfinished snonets (unfinished).docx" which T.S.R. said he believed contained "some of [his] best lines ever." I had to piece it together from fragments littered all over the document, often choosing between three or more different versions of the same line. I was eventually able to get something close to a working version together, but none of the versions of this particular line, line six, rhymed with any of the versions of line eight, as the form demanded. It wasn't until late in the process, when T.S.R. and I had established (somewhat) regular communication, that I received the following message from him at 4:36 am EST:

*Aannandndd ofofofo agagaiiannini wititht soemeomtthingingni ththtahhtat hahahaddd beenenn*

Needless to say, I was a bit put off by the spelling, the late hour, and the lack of context, but none of that was particularly out of character for T.S.R. I also quickly realized that this line, once the unusual spelling had been corrected, did happen to fit perfectly into Sonnet IV, so I added it to the manuscript. While this poem doesn't fit the obvious theme of the collection (unrequited love), T.S.R.'s extensive notes and late additions make clear that he put some deep thought into it and it meant something to him. Perhaps there is something more to these lines than it seems, waiting to be uncovered by an astute reader.

V.

The richest man on Earth is Elon Musk[6]
(Or so they say) but does he truly feel
At peace with life or is he just a husk
Who doesn't see in riches much appeal?
My guess is that he's happy, since he's rich,
And people who are wealthy often are
Beloved by everyone around them, which
Is nice, I would imagine from afar.
One day, I'll be as rich as Elon is,
And I will purchase Amazon from him,[7]
And buy a bunch of fancy palaces,
And fly to Okinawa on a whim.
        But here's a promise I am certain of:
        That I will split these riches with my love.

---

[6] The richest man on Earth is Jeff Bezos.

[7] T.S.R. seems to have conflated the accomplishments and reputations of Elon Musk and Jeff Bezos into a single person. This cleverly plays into what I believe is a central theme in his work: the depersonalization that comes with great wealth. While T.S.R. often asserts that wealth is the source of great happiness, he also slyly undermines his own premise by conceding that the value of wealth pales in comparison to the value of friendship and romantic love.

While assembling the final manuscript, I did send T.S.R. a brief note inquiring as to whether this was his intention, and never received a clear answer. I must admit that communication with the author was difficult, as I will explain later.

VI.

The way the soundboard echoes with the pitch
Of hammered string; the way the windchime sings
To life the voiceless longing and the rich
Inflection of the wind; the way dawn brings
A symphony of birds transforming light
To sound; the way the silence of the air
Is somehow audible, heard from the height
Of mountain peaks where one would never dare
To climb alone; the way a water drop
Is multiplied by echoes in the deep
Part of a cave; the way desires swap
Themselves for sounded murmurs when asleep
    Is just the way my heartbeat echoes through
    My body when I catch a glimpse of you.[8]

---

[8] As I have mentioned before, I pride myself on my relatively light hand as an editor. I feel it is my job only to polish the gems of the author's imagination, never to impose my own will or beliefs onto their work. However, I did make a number of small changes to this sonnet. In the initial draft, a few words were missing, with nonsense placeholders left in. "Hammered," for example, was represented by "doobie," and "symphony" by "boobiedoop." This is of course, a fairly standard practice for poets who work in strict metered forms. There were also a number of words that seemed off, but the replacement was so obvious that I just made the change myself. "Audible" was originally "hearable," and "peaks" was originally "one slyable for top of mountain idk?" The final word of the poem was inexplicably "thou" instead of "you," which does not rhyme, and is not used anywhere else in the collection.

I made these changes and sent them to the author for approval. He responded immediately (a rarity for T.S.R.), writing, "I don't see any changes."

Perhaps this is the poem that he saw in his mind's eye all along? Often when working with the most brilliant writers, I notice that their imaginations can sometimes leap ahead of their pens, and certain words get skipped over as they after the fleeting quarry that is inspiration. Based on his reaction, I feel confident that the editorial liberties I occasionally took would be viewed by T.S.R. (if he ever gets around to reading the finished manuscript—not sure he will, more on that later) not as the imposition of my own agenda upon his work, but as a careful excavation of what was contained in the work all along.

VII.

The school-bell rings,[9] announcing end of day,
And all the other boys rush out of class.
They joke around, and call each other "gay,"
Which shouldn't be an insult, but alas!
There is a part of me that wants to be
A part of them, however coarse and crude
Their sense of humor is, to have them see
Me as an equal, call me "bro" or "dude."
But I could never be accepting of
All of their homophobic turns of phrase.
I think people should love whoe'er they love
Without being made fun of—even gays.
       If these boys ever felt a love that's real,
       They'd never ridicule how others feel.

---

[9] This is the first poem to explicitly reference school. T.S.R. himself does not go to school. He is, as anyone reading this is undoubtedly aware, a wealthy investor-cum-poet in his mid-to-late thirties-plus. It is all the more impressive, then, how effectively he is able to adopt the persona of an insecure teenager in his exploration of the near-universal experience of unrequited love.

VIII.

He trips me on my way across the quad[10]
And calls me names that I shall not repeat.
He says I'll never have a rockin' bod
And claims my muscles look like Cream of Wheat.
Yet I can sense the pain behind the jabs
For I have known him longer than most others,
And though he now makes jokes about my abs,
There was a time when we were almost brothers.
Before his mom divorced his dad we told
Each other everything like best friends do.
We played Nintendo, sometimes even bowled.
I told him of the love I bear for you.
    So though he's now a bully, we can't part
    For he's the only soul who knows my heart.

---

[10] Actually, on the topic of school, I also want to briefly mention one particular exchange we had, where I sent him an email containing a minor editorial question. The email ended, as all of my professional emails do, with a signature containing both my professional email address and personal phone number. I had also included this information in the bodies of multiple emails, and reiterated to T.S.R. that he could contact me directly via email or phone at any time. Despite these efforts, he chose to communicate with me exclusively via the contact form on the publisher's website (sootspritebooks.com). This meant our conversations were never consolidated into chronological email threads, and it was often difficult to ascertain which question he was answering on the rare occasion that he did respond in answer to one of my questions. To this particular question he responded (or *seemed* to respond I should say, though it's possible he was responding to another thread of conversation [see previous sentence]) in his typically eccentric style, "Srory I actually have to go to detnetion today but I'll lookat this later."

It makes one wonder if, despite being an established adult (see note 9), his imagination was so rich that by embracing an adolescent mode of thinking and feeling for the purposes of writing these poems, he actually began on a certain level to believe himself to be an actual adolescent with an actual detention. I can imagine him disappearing into a kind of writerly fantasy world, imbued with the excesses of youthful romance through which he would frolic, plucking the sweetest fruits of literary imagining, and letting standard communication fall slightly by the wayside. This often happens when one is writing poetry, in my experience.

T.S.R., if you ever read this (which you probably won't, more on that later), I hope you did get a chance to consider the editorial question I asked on July 1, 2021 (see first paragraph) and that you approve of the changes I made. If you disagree with my changes, please contact me via phone or email (or the contact form on the publisher's website sootspritebooks.com, though I would really prefer phone or email) and let me know, so that we can revise for the second edition (assuming that the first run sells out, which I imagine it will based solely on the strength of the poems).

IX.

Is there an artist anywhere on Earth[11]
Skillful enough to capture how you look?
I personally think your beauty's worth
A better portrait than my sketching-book
So far contains, although I really try.
I practice drawing twice or thrice a day
And conjure you often in my mind's eye
In detail, and I think that you could say
That I'm improving. Still, it's not enough.
I tried to draw you in a Ghibli style,
But honestly it came out pretty rough.
I'll try again after a little while.
    And then I'll try again, and then again,
    Until I am the master of the pen.

---

[11] Sorry, I kind of ran out of space on the last page, so I have to put this here. The editorial question I was talking about (see note 10, paragraphs 1 and 3) was regarding the use of certain pronouns throughout the collection. My best estimation is that the collection centers on two subjects (once again, cleverly reflecting Shakespeare's own Sonnets, which split their attention between the "dark lady" and the "fair youth") referred to as "you" and "he." "You" seems quite clearly to be the subject of the protagonist's admiration, while "he" (referenced in Sonnet VIII, for example), seems to be a kind of bully character from the protagonist's youth. This of course plays into the cycle's recurring theme of adolescence, firmly placing the collection in the great Germanic tradition of *schulromane*, (an unjustly neglected subgenre of the *bildungsroman*).

However, while I was piecing together some of the unfinished sonnets (see note 8, but also more on that later), I began to feel as if there were perhaps some other character being referenced in certain lines. It seems silly to think about, now that the collection is complete, but I wanted to make sure there wasn't some third stream of narrative energy hidden in the poems that I had failed to pick up on. I edited the collection assuming that there were only the two subjects I had initially identified, and that's the decision for which I was seeking T.S.R.'s approval via email (see previous note). There is more that I could say, but my hope is to keep these notes as concise as possible, as you will have noticed, so I will save it for another page.

## X.

The reservations and uncertainties
That creep around the edges of a thought
Are sometimes paralyzing. All of these
Annoying feelings really are a lot.[12]
If I'd instead been born a robot-boy
I wouldn't feel so many things at once,
And when I fell in love I could enjoy
The feeling without acting like a dunce.
But on the other hand, the wisest sages
Have often said that robots cannot feel.
They never have depressions, joys, or rages,
Because their robot hearts aren't truly real.
    I'm fine with feeling bad sometimes, it's true,
    As long as I can still feel love for you.

---

[12] This line was originally, "Annoying feelings really are *too much*," (emphasis mine) which rhymed with the earlier versions of line two. However, I felt that line two in other drafts never really "sang" the way that the rest of the poem did, and I wrote T.S.R., wondering if there was an updated version. He did not respond (at least not directly, more on that in the following sentence). It wasn't until a couple of weeks later that I received a note through the contact form on the publisher's website sootspritebooks.com just after three in the morning Eastern time.

I don't remember if I mentioned this already, but about halfway through the editing process, T.S.R. suddenly got in the habit of contacting me at extremely odd hours, sending me single lines or occasionally rhyming couplets with extremely odd spelling. (*Editor's note: I actually did mention it already [see note 5]. I'll be sure to revise this passage for the second edition.*)

One of the earliest messages he sent to me in this fashion contained only the following text, with no explanation:

*ththatht creeppep arorordoudndn thehe eeddgggesss offf aa thotuuguhtt*

It struck me like a bolt of lightning that this was the perfect line to replace line two in this sonnet, and I changed the ending words of line four to make it rhyme. (T.S.R. if you're reading this [which you probably aren't {more on that later}], I await your feedback with an open heart.)

I did, of course, momentarily consider the possibility that this line wasn't intended to be a part of these "unrequited love" sonnets, and was in fact a piece of some separate narrative stream, but I quickly brushed that possibility aside when I discovered how beautifully it fit into Sonnet X.

## XI.

I never was a fan of basketball—
It seemed to me like any other sport—
Until the day my eyes beheld your tall
And graceful figure bounding 'cross the court.
Your shorts of polyester shimmering,
Your close-cropped hair bouncing upon your head,
You caught the ball and started dribbling—
I sat and dreamed that one day we should wed.
You're probably the strongest high-school student[13]
I've ever seen. Your prowess makes me wonder[14]
If working out more often would be prudent,[15]
Until I, too, have huge triceps of thunder.[16]
        One day I'll be as cool and strong as you
        And then, perhaps, you'll come to love me too.

---

[13] See note 14

[14] See note 15

[15] See note 16

[16] In classical verse, the addition of an unstressed eleventh syllable to a pentametrical line is called a "feminine ending." Here, T.S.R. utilizes four of these such "feminine endings" in a row. This should obviously be a clue to the "feminine" quality of the subject of the poem, i.e. that "you" refers to a female love interest.

Once again paralleling Shakespeare, T.S.R. seems to have built his sonnet cycle around two subjects: one female, one male. This makes me more confident in my editorial choice to interpret the "you" and the "he" in the manner that I did (see note 11).

(*Editor's note: I did, much later in the process, have some reason to doubt this decision, but more on that later.*)

XII.

If I could chart my income on a graph
And show it to you, (lines and bars and such)
Would it attract you, or would you just laugh,
And say "this doesn't matter very much?"
If I could take the stocks I've gained and lost
And organize them spreadsheetwise for you
Between two points of knowing is the cost[17]
Of feeling so in love, what would you do?
I always have assumed that you'd prefer
To date me if I had a bunch of dough,
Cause girls like money, or so I infer.
That's kind of an unfair assumption though.
        If you should ever fall in love with me,
        I hope it's for my personality.

---

[17] This line was originally "And show you in financial terms the cost." The line I have replaced it with was sent to me after midnight (as had become T.S.R.'s habit [see notes 5 and 12]) rendered thusly:

*betetweeenn totowowo ponionts foofof knownowiwongn giss the coosost*

The original line obviously makes more sense grammatically, but this was the only place I could make the new line fit. As our correspondence went on, the late-night missives came more and more frequently, crackling with a kind of urgency that made me feel I must find a way to include each and every one of them, but more on that later.

XIII.

I wonder if he really is as strong
As he pretends to be, or if it's just
An act that he has kept up for so long
That he now feels that he forever must.
I've never seen him lifting any weights
Or posting pictures of his muscles flexed
Although he says he often goes on dates
With girls that he has courted via text.
He tells me that his push-up game is off
The hook and when I say that mine is too,
He can't contain a ridiculing scoff
And loudly tells me he thinks that's not true
        But maybe this is all a way to hide
        The loneliness he always feels inside.[18]

---

[18] Sorry, I forgot what I was going to say here. It's a very nice poem, though.

(*Editor's note: I should mention that I actually think all of the poems are nice. I don't want to leave the impression that I'm playing favorites [for more on my thoughts regarding the poems, see notes 1–46]*)

## XIV.

There are a thousand critters in my brain
That waken in the deep part of a dream[19]
Tapping against my mind's eye's windowpane
And when I rouse the morning after seem[20]
To settle down a bit, at least compared
To how insane they acted in the night.
At night it's like I get the crazies squared
But the next day, I guess that it's alright.
Am I the only one who feels this way?
There's got to be a couple other dudes,
At least, who can keep calm during the day,
But then at night misplace a bunch of foods.
        One day if I get married, this will take
        Explaining for my wife or husband's sake.

---

[19] See note 20

[20] The great difficulty of editing this collection was piecing together complete poems from the multiple incomplete drafts in multiple documents which T.S.R. (kindly) provided me. This is one such poem. While most of it came from the aforementioned "unfinished snonets (unfinished).docx," (see note 5 paragraph 1) lines two and four were sent to me late at night (see notes 5, 12, and 17), spelled like so:

*Hthhthatht wwakkakekenen inn theeh deeppe apaprpat fofof aa adreamamamm*

*Naanndndnnd whhehhene hyououoou roruoousoueo ehtehhe meornrnirinign afftere seeem*

In addition to fixing the spelling of these lines, I also had to change the pronoun "you" in the second line to "I" to make it work in the context of Sonnet XIV. As we have established, "you" consistently refers to the beloved, and "I" to the protagonist. I'm not sure why he would have changed that convention here, unless there is some other "you" to whom T.S.R. has yet to introduce the reader (a remote possibility, but more on that later).

XV.

You lift an arm from out the swimming pool
And water-droplets streak across your skin.
They catch the light like facets of a jewel[21]
Or th'piles of gold that Scrooge McDuck swims in.
The doctor says I shouldn't go near water
At least until my fascia has regrown
So from the bleachers at our Alma Mater
I live through you (and film you on my phone).
It's not like I do anything uncouth
With all these videos I have of you.
I rarely look at them, to tell the truth,
Except when I am feeling really blue.
        Y'know, I guess this does sound kind of weird.
        I'll go delete the vids where you've appeared.

---

[21] I have mentioned before (see notes 2, 7, 8, 10, and 12) that he became difficult to communicate with—it's not that he stopped contacting me entirely (not for a while at least, more on that later), but that the messages he sent were unfailingly off-topic, and often of a bizarrely personal nature to which I felt ill-equipped to respond ("Do dyou love your parents?" "Do you nedd real freidns if you're propular on yotube?" "How does osmoen know if tyehr'e a lesbian?"). There were certain points where it seemed, much to my dismay, that he had lost interest entirely in his poetry collection. Then I would wake up the next morning to find that a single line of perfectly rendered (though bafflingly misspelled) iambic pentameter had arrived through the contact form of our website sootspritebooks.com. But more on that later.

## XVI.

What do you think about when you're alone?
Do you get lost in worlds of afterthought?[22]
And do you wish for someone to have known
That day the things that you wish you forgot?
Are you as confident as your short hair
And pastel goth accessories suggest?
And do you walk around without a care,
Or is there more to you than I have guessed?
I think there's prob'ly more to you than I
Had thought there was before which is how come
I've had a crush on you since junior high.
You seem so smart. I prob'ly seem so dumb.
      If there were secrets you wished to confide
      I'd keep them for you til the day I died.

---

[22] I must admit again to having made an alteration. This poem was pieced together from multiple drafts, but line two was incomplete in all of them. I completed it myself (adding the phrase "worlds of afterthought") after I received line four late one night (originally "ththahaht tdaayy thee ththiingnngns thhtaht youo wwishshsh youou foorogoogotot" (see notes 5, 12, 17, and 20) and recognized it as an opportunity to complete this fragment.

XVII.

This morning in geometry I used
A compass that I grabbed from Teacher's drawer
To draw a perfect circle. It amused
Me, so I went and drew a couple more.
The pencil tip, it swings around the point
Which guides it in its course around and round
The same way my love for you does anoint
You as the center to which I am bound.
A simple glance can make a moment good
A bit more often than would otherwise[23]
Have happened, and the other things that would
Have been the case and all the time that lies[24]
       Around the circle is where I belong,
       But then the bell rings and I say, "so long."

---

[23] See note 24

[24] This poem was altered slightly by the editor (*Editor's note: me*) and published in this form pending T.S.R.'s approval (he hasn't responded, but I have faith that he will before we print the second edition). Although I am the one who assembled the lines into their final order, I must reiterate that T.S.R. is responsible for their composition and I was only trying to honor what I assumed must have been his intentions (he had become at this point exceedingly difficult to communicate with, see note 21).

I mention this because line ten (see note 23) and line twelve (see current note) were among the late-night missives I have already described (see notes 5, 12, 17, 20, and 22), and were not a part of the original draft of this poem. It's true that the final sentence, with these additions in place, does become a bit of a run-on, and seems to shift in tone and focus in a way that is difficult to follow, but in the opinion of the editor (*Editor's note: me again*) it creates a kind of dreamy, late-night, stream-of-consciousness quality that I came to believe was integral to T.S.R.'s artistic vision, but more on that later.

XVIII.[25]

Just how much would I pay to reconvene
Upon that grassy hill where you and I
Once sat and talked, and almost did I lean
Upon your muscled shoulder with a sigh;
The hillside where this question did you pose:
"So anyway, do you like anyone?
Like them like them I mean," and my heart rose
To think our love could finally be begun.
But then, for reasons that I still don't know,
I couldn't bring myself to say a word.
You smiled at me and said, "I get it, bro,"
As if in silence, some secret you heard.
   If I could go back and redo that day,
   What would I find the courage then to say?

---

[25] Speaking of the "dreamy, late-night, stream-of-consciousness quality" which I referenced in note 24 (see note 24), it feels worth mentioning that it is currently 4:36 am, the exact time at which I received the first "late-night missive" from T.S.R. (see note 5). I'm not normally a "night-owl," to use that terribly gauche phrase, but receiving T.S.R.'s wee-hours iambic dispatches was so exhilarating that at a certain point I found myself lying awake in bed in anticipation, wondering if tonight could be the night that I receive another one. (*Editor's note: By "tonight" I mean the hypothetical "tonight" during which I was having the aforementioned thought, not the actual, current "tonight" during which it's 4:36 am [Editor's note: scratch that, 4:37 am] and I'm finalizing my annotations.*) At a certain point it became useless to pretend that I would sleep at all during the night, so I would stay up to pore over T.S.R.'s piecemeal drafts and await his mysterious additions.

XIX.

I wrote a poem about you yesterday—
But not this poem, a different one, I mean—
It started with, "Just how much would I pay,"
And then the next words were, "To reconvene…"
I'm thinking that that poem would be a good
Example of my writing[26] if I ever
Decide to show you. I hope that you would
Think that it's nice and that the rhymes are clever.
And by the way, in case you ever read
These poems and wonder if when I say "you"
That "you" is really you, yourself, I need
To just confess that, yeah, it is, it's true.
        You are the you that all of these poems mention.
        I guess I'll see you later in detention.

---

[26] I don't know if I can properly describe the thrill of refreshing my inbox and seeing there waiting for me a message (sent through the contact form on the publisher's website sootspritebooks.com) from T.S. (if he would allow me the privilege of calling him by his first name). It's not that I was lonely while assembling these poems (*Editor's note: nor am I lonely now, as I rush to finish these annotations in time for publication*), but I had just moved across the country to New York City chasing after a dream of mine (there's no need to divulge what the dream itself actually was, as I believe an editor's own personal feelings have no place in commentary such as this) and as the reader (*Editor's note: you*) can probably imagine, it can be a strain on one's soul to be in a new city carving out a new life with few if any social contacts. (*Editor's note: I mean in-person social contacts. I am of course active on social media as well as through the publisher's website sootspritebooks.com.*) And occasionally, amidst the bleariness, a message from T.S. Roach would shine into my inbox.

## XX.

If I appear to you throughout the day
And night in passing, even when you try
To focus thoughts on things your teachers say
Should ratherly your mind's eye occupy;
If things you used to love seem less and less
Worth doing by yourself, and so you dream
Of having someone with you just to bless
The moment with their presence and esteem;
If future thinkings take you by the hand
And lead you in a dreaming state to where
We two can sometime be together and
The dreams divide into the cooling air[27]
        Then come with me to fly across the fault[28]
        Remember and to peer inside the vault[29]

---

[27] The feeling was something like the moment when you first kick off your flip-flops and press your heel into hot, dry sand at the beach except if the sound was the feeling and the feeling was the sound, and both of them were actually an emotion that spread across the back of your neck and had nothing to do with feet or sand at all. "Tthehehe ddreaammss didiiviviiddee inntotot thee cooollign aiaiiririr," I would read, and somewhere waves would crash onto a shore.

[28] Occasionally the late-night lines arrived as rhyming couplets, and even more occasionally, providence allowed that I could keep them together, as here (see note 29).

[29] And then it was like pressing both heels into the sand, at the very same time, if one could do so without losing one's balance (again, metaphorically [see note 27, first sentence]).

## XXI.

There was a time not long ago when he
And I arrived in class before the rest.
We talked like it was almost normal. We
Discussed both being nervous for a test.
We normally don't talk except at gym
He lives in hours out of time and where[30]
A part of you; and you a part of him[31]
Would steal my towel and sometimes underwear.
The song of him to listen to the song[32]
Because he lives only because of you[33]
To listen and to carry him along[34]
And one time in preschool, we both ate glue.
    Will we one day be friends like this again?
    Perhaps the day will come, when we're old men.

---

[30] But what was most maddening of all was the feeling of only ever knowing one small part of a person. When T.S. and I were initially put in contact and I received the first few poems, I felt an immense closeness with this person I had never met.

[31] I recognized something behind the lines, and also felt somehow that the lines themselves recognized me. I ached to spend time with them, to spend time with him, to crack open the cosmic shell of his consciousness and sip from the sweet yolk inside. (*Editor's note: Sorry if that metaphor was unclear. We don't eat eggs in my family, so I don't actually know how it works.*)

[32] For a time I was able to do just that. But then our communications reached a dead end, and all I was left with was a deluge of esoteric lines in inscrutable spellings arriving at odd hours. I read and reread them. I did the best I could, but the more I read and considered and rearranged, the more I brimmed with questions, and the one man who could answer them would not.

[33] I had long assumed that all the "he"s and "him"s of the collection referred to the same friend-cum-rival whom I was able to picture so clearly while reading the early poems. Late in the process of ordering and completing the collection I was left with this exasperating set of late-night lines (see notes 30 through 34), all referencing a "he" or a "him," and so I put them together as sensibly as I could with other friend-cum-rival fragments and I feel that I have done a respectable job, but what if this "he" is not that "he"? What if the continuity I have worked to preserve is just one among many un-checked assumptions?

[34] If T.S. were still in the habit of responding, I would ask him: Who is the "he" who "lives in hours out of time"? Who is the "you" who "never should have seen and known" (more on that later)? And who is the I who reads and arranges and annotates all of these lines and what am I hoping will come of it? Who am I? Who is anyone? T.S. if you read this please get back to me soon. I would like these questions sorted out prior to the release of the second edition.

XXII.[35]

I still remember when you cut your hair
From long to short and then showed up at school
And walked around and didn't seem to care
If anybody thought that you were cool—
Which made you even cooler, IMO,
Because it's cool to seem like you don't care.
And when that girl said you looked like a ho,
You smiled and walked off like she wasn't there.
I wish I could be confident like that.
Though no one's ever called me "ho," it's true,
I got made fun of when I wore a hat
To school that showed the hot guy from Haikyuu.
        One day, together, we shall walk away
        From all the mean things that our bullies say.

---

[35] Sorry, I just need a minute.

XXIII.

The beauty of a cloudless summer sky,
The brightness of a radiant full moon,
The outfit on a fashionable guy,
Are nothing next to you for whom I swoon.
Remember then the song to listen to[36]
And I will hold safely for you until[37]
Between the eyelids that divide in two[38]
You if you let them and one day you will[39]
Forget completely, you cannot implant[40]
Things that you never should have seen and known[41]
Sky beckons you from dreaming, but you can't[42]
Too soon the truth of all that is to own[43]
        The beauteousness that you have is such
        That even other beaut'ful things can't touch.

---

[36] Okay, I'm back.

[37] Sorry about disappearing.

[38] I'm fine now, though. I took a little walk around my apartment and had a glass of water, and I feel much better.

[39] Except that I stubbed my toe. It always takes a few minutes for my eyes to adjust to the darkness after I've been looking at this document for too long.

[40] Sorry, I was supposed to mention that the lines noted in notes 36 through 43 were all late night additions.

[41] See note 40.

[42] See note 40.

[43] See note 40.

XXIV.

I wonder when I see you looking out
Again the way you shouldn't have to do
The clouds or if you ever think about
My own reflection looking back at you.
The worlds of losing and remembering
Look like a bluish ghost, pencil in hand
And when you are able again to sing
Far off in an imagined magic land
I made up in my mind and other things
And in pianos, in pauses between
A person who is like you but who brings
The hummings of the strings and you have seen
      Of this to feel relief of what was lost.
      My mom takes out some chicken to defrost.[44]

---

[44] It's getting very late (or early [although I suppose it's always getting either late or early {especially lately the way that days and nights seem to run together in a haze on the periphery around the computer screen where I stare and stare and try to decode these remaining verses}]) and the hour at which this manuscript is due is itself only an hour away, so I will try to wrap things up quickly. There was a certain point in the process when I was left only with the barest fragments, some from earlier documents, and some received late at night through the contact form on the publisher's website sootspritebooks.com with no explanation (see notes 5, 12, 17, 20, 22, 23, 24, 27, 28, 29, 30, 31, 32, 33, 34, 36, 37, 38, 39, 40, 41, 42, and 43) and no indication of how I was to string them together. After weeks (at least I think it was weeks, but really how is one supposed to know how much time elapses between one now and another?) of working on this project, combing through words for tints and shades of meaning, I was left with a jumble that I could make no meaning out of, and so I had to abandon the search for understanding and instead let the rhyme scheme guide me because if we can't have truth at least we can still have rhyme.

XXV.[45]

The memories you feared would overtake
Relief with all things living wanders in
Apart from who you would be while awake
Who carried you before the pseudonym
You planted to escape to; where you clove
Some story that you would prefer instead
Took root and grew beyond the little grove
Of hurtful things that echo in your head
Like something you imagined, something you
A thing that is not light or dark in poor
Could shake away like dewdrops when the blue
Is not a thing at least too long before
        If just to let the morning see you smile
        And so I take them only for a while

---

[45] And then every fragment was accounted for and I thought my work was finished, but the late-night lines (see all notes referenced in note 44) continued, night after night and so I returned to my charge ordering and reordering them until meaning gave way completely, and then eventually even rhyme itself crumbled. (*Editor's note: I take full responsibility for the imperfect "slant" rhyme between lines 2 and 4 which you have undoubtedly noticed, and which I am certain would go against the intentions of the artist, a man with a virtually unparalleled gift for verse, but I cannot ask him about his intentions because he has stopped responding to my messages as I will explain later.*) I keep asking myself, was there a better way to do this? Are patterns laced through the words that could have revealed themselves to a more discerning eye? Or am I just thinking too hard about things because I haven't slept in so long that thinking too hard about things is all I have left? The morning cock is soon to crow (*Editor's note: by morning cock I actually mean the street sweepers which pass loudly by my apartment every Monday morning, rattling the windows and shaking me from my slumber [or, lately, from one wakefulness to another]. There are no morning cocks in New York City [that I know of] at least not in the part of the city where I live, but maybe in Staten Island somewhere, which I have never visited and imagine to be mostly agricultural*) and this document is due in less than an hour (and less and less and less than that with every passing second).

XXVI.

and listen, and remember, and listen, and remember,
and listen, and remember[46]

---

[46] These two lines were the second to last piece of correspondence I received from T.S.R. The final piece came the following day, when in desperation I emailed him, "WHAT DO I DO WITH THESE?" He responded (promptly, contrary to my expectations), "im busy ahnnging out with my frined today ill look at tihs later," and that was the last I heard from him.

I do not know if he lost interest in the collection, or if he was unsatisfied with my work as editor, or if I offended him with the interrogatory tone of my all-caps email. I do know that if he ever returns to complete this project, the final eight sonnets are sure to shimmer with unparalleled glory. For the time being, we can only imagine the kind of Parnassian gymnastics Sonnets XX-VII-XXXIV must contain, wherever they are (some forgotten notebook, or notepad, or a drawer in the backroom of the poet's imagination, or that earlier, unseen plane where poems gestate before being born). I think I have some more thoughts to share, but I can't hear them over the blare of the street sweeper, so I will end by saying that my only real hope is that my dear T.S.R., poet laureate of heartache, is happy hanging out with his friend, whoever and wherever they may be.

# Afterword

Hi. It's Sarah again. I'll bet you weren't expecting an afterword for this collection. Readers, nor was I. In an effort not to get sued or involved in a police investigation, I am submitting in writing that Kevin Y is okay. He is fine, you guys. As I've said before, he is an upstanding, passionate literary citizen. But I was not aware of the intense level of sheer…dedication he was giving to this book until I read the whole fever dream of it during what I thought would be a rudimentary final check before transmittal. Hoo, boy. I mean…you just read it, so you know. I called him right away. His voice sounded thin, somehow stale and new, like he hadn't tried it in a while. I asked the things a responsible adult is supposed to: how are you doing, what's on your mind, have you been eating, have you been sleeping. The answer to everything was "no," even when it didn't make sense. Long story short, he is now asleep on the couch in my apartment, and I am in his, catsitting and messing with these files at the last possible dang minute.

I wanted to clear up a couple of other things, too. One is: I don't know where Kevin Y got the idea that Soot Sprite would do a second edition of this book. They can't promise a second edition of a paperback before having sold even a single copy of the first edition. That is just not a thing. Another is: It's true; there are only twenty-six sonnets, not thirty-four.

Lastly: Kevin Y was despondent over something to do with the "extra lines" sent via the contact form at sootspritebooks.com. These are well documented in the text itself and I had hoped to wrap things up and set any lingering questions aside—but found myself strangely drawn in by the fact of their unconventional transmission and Kevin Y's various theories on what it all could mean. I have puzzled over and rearranged these (ignoring several voicemails from production and who knows how many emails at this point). Curiously, despite T.S. Roach's stated goal to write a collection of sonnets, these extra lines work best (in this editor's humble opinion) in couplets, not quatrains. I began to understand Kevin Y's sleepless study. Why break your own rules for your own collection, as though some other author took the reins? What was T.S. Roach's intention with these free-floating lines, if he had any intention at all? They could have been submitted by anyone—were they really sent by him? (But if not him, who else? And why?) We will most likely never have answers to these questions, but my heart tells me that the author, or whoever or whatever wrote these lines, would want them out there in the world, together. For the curious reader, here is my best attempt at arranging them. Make of this what you will. Stockadoodledoo, or something.

> he lives in hours out of time and where
> the dreams divide into the cooling air
> and in pianos, in pauses between
> the hummings of the strings and you have seen
> things that you never should have seen and known
> too soon the truth of all that is to own
> is not a thing at least too long before
> a thing that is not light or dark in poor
> relief with all things living wanders in
> and off again with something that had been
> a part of you; and you a part of him
> who carried you before the pseudonym
> took root and grew beyond the little grove
> you planted to escape to; where you clove
> apart from who you would be while awake
> the memories you feared would overtake
> you if you let them and one day you will
> and I will hold safely for you until

that day the things that you wish you forgot,
that creep around the edges of a thought,
that waken in the deep parts of a dream
and when you rouse the morning after seem
like something you imagined, something you
could shake away like dewdrops when the blue
sky beckons you from dreaming, but you can't
forget completely, you cannot implant
some story that you would prefer instead
of hurtful things that echo in your head
and so I take them only for a while
if just to let the morning see you smile
a bit more often than would otherwise
have been the case and all the time that lies
between two points of knowing is the cost
of this to feel relief of what was lost
because he lives only because of you
between the eyelids that divide in two
the worlds of losing and remembering
and when you are able again to sing
the song of him to listen to the song
to listen and to carry him along
again the way you shouldn't have to do
remember then the song to listen to
then come with me to fly across the fault
remember and to peer inside the vault
and listen, and remember, and listen, and remember,
and listen, and remember.

# About the Author

**T.S. Roach** did not turn in a bio in time for publication.

# About the Editor

**Kevin Y** did not turn in a bio in time for publication.

www.ingramcontent.com/pod-product-compliance
Lightning Source LLC
Chambersburg PA
CBHW032338300426
44109CB00041B/1280